It's Not Catching

Stings & Bites

Heinemann Library
Chicago, Illinois

Angela Royston

© 2004 Heinemann Library
a division of Reed Elsevier Inc.
Chicago, Illinois

Customer Service 888-454-2279

Visit our website at www.heinemannlibrary.com

Designed by Dave Oakley, Arnos Design
Originated by Dot Gradations Ltd.
Printed and bound in China
by South China Printing Company

08 07 06 05 04
10 9 8 7 6 5 4 3 2 1

**Library of Congress
Cataloging-in-Publication Data**
Royston, Angela.
   It's not catching stings and bites / Angela
Royston.   v. cm.
Includes bibliographical references and index.
Contents: What are stings and bites? -- Who gets stings and bites? -- Stinging insects -- Jellyfish and sea urchins -- Mosquitoes -- Spiders and snakes -- Dogs and other animals -- What happens when you are stung or bitten? -- Getting help -- Antidotes for serious bites or stings -- Preventing mosquito bites -- Be careful. ISBN 1-4034-4826-4 (hbk.) 1. Bites and stings--Juvenile literature. [1. Bites and stings.] I. Title: Stings and bites. II. Title.
   RD96.2.R69 2004
   617.1--dc22

                                        2003019819

Acknowledgments
The author and publishers are grateful to the following for permission to reproduce copyright material: p. 4 SPL/ Dr John Brackenbury; p. 5 Tudor Photography; p. 6 (top), 23 Getty Images; pp. 6 (bottom), 20, 26 Phillip James Photography; p. 7 SPL/Gusto; p. 8 SPL; pp. 9, 18, 21, 22, 25 Trevor Clifford; p. 10 Getty Images/John Warden; p. 11 Getty Images/Taxi/Peter Atkinson; p. 12 Getty Images/LSHTM; p. 13 Still Pictures; p. 14 Getty Images/Buddy Mays; p. 15 Getty Images/Tom Bean; p. 16 Alamy/Bob Elsdale; p. 17 Getty Images/American Images Inc; p. 19 SPL/Dr Paul Marazzi; p. 24 SPL/Mauro Fermariello; p. 27 Getty Images/Fran May; p. 28 Getty Images/ Martin Bydalek; p. 29 Getty Images/Lo Adamski Peeke.

Cover photograph reproduced with permission of Trevor Clifford.

The publishers would like to thank David Wright for his assistance in the preparation of this book.

Every effort has been made to contact copyright holders of any material reproduced in this book. Any omissions will be rectified in subsequent printings if notice is given to the publisher.

Contents

Some words are shown in bold, **like this.** You can find out what they mean by looking in the glossary.

What Are Stings and Bites?

A sting or a bite is an animal's way of keeping itself safe. For example, a **hornet** stings when it is attacked. It can use its **stinger** to sting both people and animals.

Other animals use their teeth to bite their enemies. Pets, such as hamsters, are usually safe to pick up. But they may bite if they are afraid or have babies to protect.

Who Gets Stings and Bites?

Most kinds of **insects** and other animals do not bite or sting. But some insects and other animals bite or sting any person that scares or bothers them.

You are most likely to be bitten or stung
if you trap or step on an animal, such as this
scorpion. You cannot catch a bite or sting
from another person.

Stinging Insects

The most common stinging **insects** are wasps and bees. They have a **stinger** on the end of their bodies that they push into your skin. Some insects leave the stinger in your skin.

8

Poison flows
down the stinger
into your skin.
The bee dies soon
afterwards. Some
insects do not lose
their stinger and can
sting you again!

Jellyfish and Sea Urchins

Some sea animals use **poison** to defend themselves or to catch **prey.** Jellyfish have stingers on their long **tentacles.** Jellyfish stings can hurt and even kill people.

A **sea urchin** has long, **poisonous** spines to protect itself from being eaten. If you step on a sea urchin, the spines will stick in your foot.

Mosquitoes

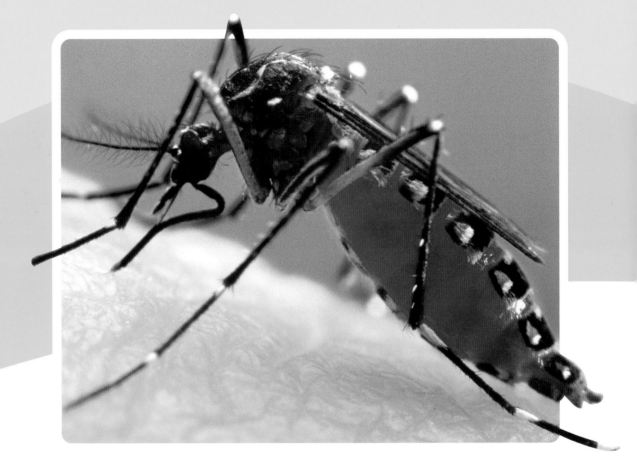

Mosquitoes are one of the most common biting **insects.** Mosquitoes feed on the blood of animals and people. When they bite, they can push **germs** into your body.

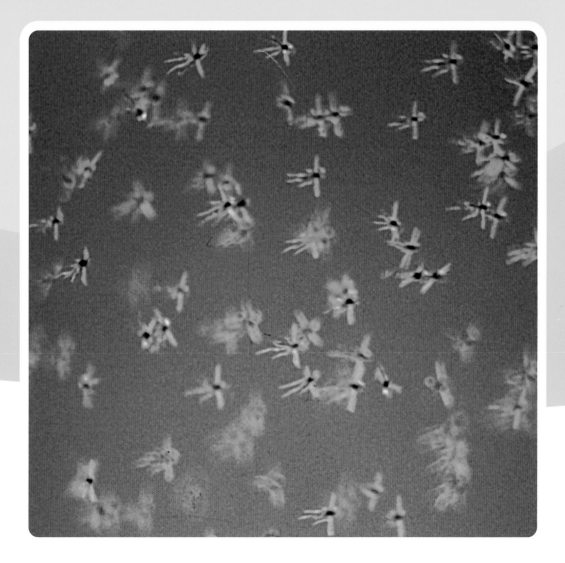

In some parts of the world, mosquitoes spread a dangerous **disease** called **malaria.** A person can only catch malaria when they are bitten by a mosquito that is carrying the disease. You cannot catch malaria from a person or an animal.

Spiders and Snakes

Spiders use their **fangs** to kill their **prey.**
The bites of some spiders are so **poisonous,**
they can make people very sick, or even kill
them. The spider in this picture is called a
black widow. It is very dangerous.

Some kinds of snakes, like this rattlesnake,
also have a poisonous bite. The snake sinks
its fangs into its prey. The **poison** then flows
into the **victim's** blood.

Dogs and Other Animals

Dogs, cats, and other animals can bite you if they are scared or angry. Pets may bite you by accident when you are playing with them.

VALLEY PARK
ELEMENTARY LIBRARY

Most animal bites are not **poisonous,** but an animal's teeth are covered in **germs.** If an animal's teeth break your skin, the germs can pass through the cut into your blood.

17

Being Stung or Bitten

It is usually easy
to tell when
you have been
stung or bitten
by an **insect.** Your
skin swells up into a small red lump.
The lump may be itchy or painful.

A tick is a small insect like a spider. When a tick bites you, it hangs on to your skin. Then, the area swells up. Ask an adult to pull out the tick using tweezers.

Treating Minor Bites and Stings

Most **insect** bites and stings can be treated by using a special cream called cortizone. The cream stops the pain, and the bite or sting heals after a few days.

If your skin is bleeding from a sting or bite, you should tell an adult. Then, wash the area with soap and rub in **antiseptic** cream. If a dog bites you, you may need a **tetanus** shot. An adult should call a doctor.

Getting Help

Sometimes the **poison** from a bad bite or sting gets into your blood and spreads through your body. If this happens, an adult should call for medical help.

The poison from a sting or bite can make
breathing difficult and make you feel sleepy.
It is very important to get help right away if
you are bitten by a dog, snake, spider, or
another insect or animal.

Treating Serious Bites and Stings

If you have been bitten by a **poisonous** snake or spider, you should see a doctor right away. It will help the doctor if you can tell him or her what the snake or spider looked like.

The doctor or **poison center** may give
you an **antivenom** shot. This is a
special medicine that stops the poison
from hurting you.

Preventing Mosquito Bites

Mosquitoes come out to feed when it gets dark. You can spray your skin with a **chemical** called bug repellent that keeps mosquitoes away.

A special type of candle called citronella makes a chemical that drives mosquitoes away. Mosquito nets over your windows or bed can also stop mosquitoes from biting you.

Be Careful!

You can prevent being bitten by some animals by staying away from them. Do not pet a strange dog, especially if it is eating or is with its puppies.

When you are walking outdoors, wear sturdy shoes to protect your feet from being bitten or stung. Look carefully before you pick something up. If a bee flies near you, keep calm and quiet. Do not swat at it or scream.

Glossary

antiseptic   substance that stops germs from growing in number

antivenom   substance that acts against the effect of poison

chemical   powerful substance

disease   illness usually caused by germs

fangs   hollow teeth that an animal uses to put poison into another animal

germs   tiny living things, such as bacteria, that can cause sickness if they get inside your body

hornet   type of wasp

insect   small animal with six legs and three body parts

malaria   sickness spread by mosquitoes in some countries

mosquito   type of insect that feeds on the blood of animals and humans

poison   substance that is harmful to the body

poison center   place where information about
poisons is given

poisonous   carrying poison

prey   animal that is eaten by another animal

sea urchin   animal that lives in the sea and has
poisonous spines

stinger   body part that an animal uses to put poison
into another animal

tentacles   long feelers

tetanus   sickness that affects the muscles

victim   person or animal that is hurt or killed by
another

More Books to Read

Pascoe, Elaine. *How and Why Animals Are Poisonous.*
Huntington Beach, Calif.: Creative Teaching Press,
Inc., 2000.

Robinson, Claire. *Really Wild Snakes.* Chicago:
Heinemann Library, 1999.

Royston, Angela. *Safety First.* Chicago: Heinemann
Library, 2000.

Index